ADVANCE PRAISE FOR

Dream of the Divided Field

"Here is a book of the body, a book like no other: tender and eloquent, a singing across borders, across silences. What does it mean? It means that *Dream of the Divided Field* is a kind of book that you can't just talk about, you simply have to quote whole poems. For instance, this one: 'I woke up with so much love for you / It doesn't matter where I am // I am making eggs // The sun is warming my just-shaved head / like your hand when sometimes / it rests there.' This is because Yanyi is a terrific poet, one who's written for us a book to read when we wake in the middle of the night and need a voice that is filled with longing, truth, and delight of being, despite all the painful odds."

—Ilya Kaminsky, author of *Dancing in Odessa* and *Deaf Republic*

"Yanyi is a poet whose ambitions are soul-deep and startlingly poignant: to know the self as forever broken and to know language as the exquisite fiction of our wholeness. In his superb second book, *Dream of the Divided Field*, he recounts the dissolution of a relationship with heartbreaking clarity, revealing how the desire for reconstitution—of love, self, and world—is necessarily impossible. Yanyi knows intimately that as with the inconstancy of the lyric—queered, fragmentary, transcultural, transhistorical, pastoral, erotic, containing nothing and everything—thinking and feeling open us to the unknown and to others. Thus, the broken self is dispersed like the birds that 'fly apart and grow their understanding.' To love is to be inside and outside the self, to enter the world and let the world enter you, and how glorious it is to read a book that so bravely takes you everywhere."

—Jennifer Chang, author of *Some Say the Lark*

"Tender, alternately stark and mysterious, these poems offer a calling, a summoning, a dwelling—while also attending to wounds, scars, landscape, and surges of joy. Here, amid glorious aubades and versions of Catullus and Sappho, are intimations of a failed love, and of other impasses: a field once shared, now divided, opens onto a field of inquiry. The way one is beheld and beholds is here tested and sung. These are poems as complex homing devices; they explore shelter, alienation, microshifts in relation, sudden gusts of love. Yanyi's work is paradoxically earthily transcendental, concretely visionary. These poems move toward and through transformation. Moving between delicate lyric and poetic essai, Yanyi charts in his tremendous second book new paths for a poetry both embodied and metaphysical. Taking up one of the oldest aims of poetry, *Dream of the Divided Field* casts from its first pages a distinctive spell. It is as if the atmosphere of one's mind acquired a new coloration, or found itself an instrument newly and differently tuned."

—Maureen N. McLane, author of *Some Say* and *This Blue*

"What does it mean for each of us to be housed in a body? What is a body, but a thing to be entered and exited? In this collection of poems, Yanyi writes through leaving the body over and over—leaving old selves behind, old relationships, and old pains to birth into newness. Yanyi contends with what disappears and what stays, where we inhabit, where we can find safety, and where we can be found. A beautiful book that brings you in, that holds you close."

—Fatimah Asghar, author of *If They Come for Us*

"Not only is the field divided in these poems, it is deeply layered through a kaleidoscopic double exposure. 'The body reinventing itself became again its own mystic,' Yanyi declares in this intimate and vulnerable book. There is a before and an after: the before revealed in the memory of love and the memory of a body; and the after, a metamorphosis both corporeal and spiritual. The poems are translucent, each informs the next and echoes back—concealment followed by joyous visibility, division followed by integration, and ultimately grief transformed into a luminous reconfiguration of the self."

—Samuel Ace, author of *Meet Me There*

"A world of binaries (alive/dead, alone/together, day/night) has always been a frame—a limit to our imaginations. In order to understand oneself as separate (or separated), one must bring to mind (body, heart) the other to which one is no longer attached. In this way, there is togetherness in separation—the tether is reiterated (especially while under revision) to what was. And so how necessary, tender to experience the ever expanding multiplicity of Yanyi's exquisite *Dream of the Divided Field*, where we are reminded that 'the rain is different / each step from the moon.' Even the architecture is alive with memory, which is to say possibility. In poems that are simultaneously spare and teeming, determined and soft—'my scars enabling me to be doubly alive'—Yanyi does the patient, transcendent work of building a life larger than its loss. How grateful I am to this poet (a guide) who has shown me how to stay for a time in the irreparably gapped in order to become the building (the becoming) itself."

—TC Tolbert, co-editor of *Troubling the Line: Trans and Genderqueer Poetry and Poetics*

"'Can I come in? No, I / whisper with a voice I don't have anymore,' Yanyi writes in his new collection. That interdiction weakens as soon as it is uttered; it can't hold back the intrusions of memory, of family and lovers who insist on coming in with their own ways of seeing, their judgment or prejudice. These are to the all-seeing speaker a curse, an illumination, an opportunity, a resignation—in unequal, unpredictable measure. Perhaps as an act of survival, the speaker seems to be in all places and times at once. The kaleidoscopic vision of the poems creates a disorienting logic that animates and transforms the ordinary world, investigating the limits and multiplicities of a self."

—Saskia Hamilton, editor of *The Dolphin Letters, 1970–1979*

BY YANYI

The Year of the Blue Water
Dream of the Divided Field

Dream of the Divided Field

DREAM

of the

DIVIDED
FIELD

POEMS

YANYI

ONE WORLD
NEW YORK

Published in the United States by One World, an imprint of
Random House, a division of Penguin Random House LLC,
New York.

ONE WORLD and colophon are registered trademarks of
Penguin Random House LLC.

Some of the poems in this work have appeared, sometimes in different form, in
the following publications: "Landscape with a Hundred Turns" as part of Acad-
emy of American Poets' *Poem-a-Day*; "Taking Care" in *Bellevue Literary Review*;
"Migrants" in *Cellpoems*; "Eurydice at the Mouth" in *Memorius: A Journal of
New Verse and Fiction*; "Catullus 85," "Dream of the Divided Field," and "De-
tail" in *New England Review*; "Aubade" and "Listening to Teresa Teng" in *Res-
ervoir Journal*; "Flight" in *The Shade Journal*; "Home for the Holidays" in *West
Branch*; "Aubade (Two of Cups)" in *Already Felt: Poems in Revolt & Bounty*
(New York: Already Felt, 2021); "Family Tree" in *Queenzenglish.mp3: Poetry |
Philosophy | Performativity* (New York: Roof Books, 2020).

Grateful acknowledgment is made to HarperCollins Publishers for permis-
sion to reprint four lines from "Ars Poetica" from *New and Collected Poems:
1931–2001* by Czesław Miłosz, copyright © 1988, 1991, 1995, 2001 by Czesław
Miłosz Royalites, Inc. Used by permission of HarperCollins Publishers.

LIBRARY OF CONGRESS CATALOGING-IN-PUBLICATION DATA
Names: Yanyi (Poet), author.
Title: Dream of the divided field: poems / by Yanyi.
Description: New York: One World, [2022]
Identifiers: LCCN 2021016090 (print) |
LCCN 2021016091 (ebook) |
ISBN 9780593230992 (trade paperback; acid-free paper) |
ISBN 9780593231005 (ebook)
Subjects: LCGFT: Poetry.
Classification: LCC PS3625.A688 D74 2022 (print) |
LCC PS3625.A688 (ebook) | DDC 811/.6—dc23
LC record available at https://lccn.loc.gov/2021016090
LC ebook record available at https://lccn.loc.gov/2021016091

Printed in Canada on acid-free paper

oneworldlit.com
randomhousebooks.com

2 4 6 8 9 7 5 3 1

First Edition

Design by Fritz Metsch

*The purpose of poetry is to remind us
how difficult it is to remain just one person,
for our house is open, there are no keys in the doors,
and invisible guests come in and out at will.*

— CZESŁAW MIŁOSZ

Contents

I

In the Museum

The monument lives   inside the body.

The monument lives   outside. Two

bodies may be monuments, side by side,

enacting what is already a memory.

Move through the halls—you are styled with wings—

and pass on, constantly, while you are living.

There are no walls between the living and the dead:

only what you remember now and what you remember ahead.

Aubade (The Lake)

Buried dawn broke
onto slight leaves. And geese
between a cold and hot sky:
    a mountain and a sunrise.

It is five months since we separated.

I am not so different from the long hare
stretched by her shadow,
her spirit hanging.

What I would give for the dead
beat of mud shaped and now
eaten in. Coyotes rousing
in fast laps of the moon.

Take me to the lake and do no evil.
Lead me by the hair to who I love.

Coming Over

What was left of our relationship
neatly folded on the couch.
And the bathroom noticed
what else was missing. You
came into the bathroom, taking
out your razor, your toothbrush. Leaving
my toothbrush. Replacing every thing
next to its double, as though
I had needlessly doubled. I walked
out from my bathroom and you walked
into my bathroom. The little soap
and the razor. The duplicates in the bags
not wanting to owe me anything:

not wanting to have appeared.
It is like that. I give my house and you take
how you live in it. Not backwards or forwards,
but the past and the present
overcoming one another.

Taking Care

I take off my binder before a massage
and dream of top surgery: not having to wait

for the masseur to ask about————, my abnormal
desire to be inside this body, once, easily

identified and therefore easy to take care of.
I am not easy to take care of. I should just

take care of myself: ask a doctor to remove
the parts that are reprehensible. Like when

they break the nose in order
to construct a better one,

I bring a picture to the hairdresser. I bring
a picture to the mirror where I cut my skin

with my eyes.
As a man, I've learned something of nationhood:

the shape of a brook now straddled by a dam,
or choked by it.

Leaving the House

When I say I'm in love with you,
that means I'm not alone inside of it.

Together we talk to people
we love, separately, in one voice.

When my voice fills in love with you.
When I sing on the outside.

Transitioned

In the corner, the bodega
doesn't quite approach me.
It hides its face in its awning.

The yellow lights awake
in the taco place and, forever romantic,
on the mayo and slaw strewn on tilapia.

Eating, with new reasons, are new mouths.
The window views the third floor, which was once
my bedroom. Immersed in the view was itself.

An arch in the bathroom still remembers
my chest. How there was more
that's now lessened.

The floors had just been mopped.
Those five years taken off.

Landscape with a Hundred Turns

When you turned into a hundred rooms,
I returned each month as a door
that opened only one.

When you turned into a hundred rooms
the wind flung through
each of them wailing

and left a hundred songs
in hopes you would return for it
and me and

once, finding a doe locked up,
the trees blued up
the mountain pass, I understood

you had transformed into your multiple,
as the rain is different
each step from the moon. Sleeping

in a hundred rooms, a hundred dreams
of you appear—though by day
your voice has frozen into standing stones.

When you turned into a hundred rooms,
I met with a mirror in each eye
your growing absence.

When I moved, the shadows without you
followed me. In the hundred rooms,
I cannot pick one,

for each combines into the other
where I piece-by-piece the shadows
you have ceased

to remember. As the rain
is different each day of the year,
when I turned for you

and hoped you'd return to me,
was it I who left
and you who remained the same?

For when you changed,
I changed
the furniture in the rooms.

A hundred birds flew over a hundred fields.
A mountain flowed into a hundred rivers
then ended.

In a hundred rooms,
I turned and turned,
hoping to return to you.

O, the chrysanthemums grew
in the hundred rooms!

Far in the past and far in the future
were those numinous and echoing stars.

Aubade (In Names)

Bright One and Dear One
My Blue After Storms

My Ocean of Long Hums
My Wandering Door

My This One
My Gone One
My Lingering For

My Light One
My Long One
My Morning of More

II

Dream in Which I Try to Disappear in Front of My Aunt, or, Interrogation

I pretend to be taking a shit in the bathroom of my father's house in China. I understand this to be his house though I have never seen it before. The toilet is so close to a window that my knees touch its wall. The window is bare and plastic. I turn off the lights. My father is terrible with details, so I've spoken to him with my real voice and my real body. It's in the plastic-glass window that I see myself hiding my face in my hands, my pants down to my ankles. I wear a black silk button-down, short-sleeved with red flowers. Again, not unrecognizable as something I would claim as my own. My aunt is coming over and has attention to detail. She's coming over and I know she will tell my mother everything, so I retreat from the rooms I know she'll be in, I reverse my time. My low voice and short hair return to drawers and dark corners. She's coming over, so now I live in this bathroom, a prisoner of my father's house pretending to heave a huge shit, pretending to be in pain, pretending to be as soft as possible. She knocks. I open the bathroom door a crack, everything still to my ankles, just my nose and mouth and eyes peeking through. Can I come in? No, I whisper with a voice I don't have anymore. I am hopeful that my difference blends in, that years of being overseas can overcome the transformation. My aunt who stands at the door I won't open. My aunt whose face I worry I won't be able to draw in the dark.

Getting Around (the Dream)

I am afraid of running into you,
of having to see you,
of having to talk.

It is not clear from the dream
what I was concerned about anymore:
there was a baby involved. There was something
I didn't want.

A big house you now live in. The subways far away.
The dream makes everyone demonic but can't help anyone.
The dream is just the frame. It can't help itself.

Family Tree

I was born on October 1, 1980, in Guangzhou, China. My mother walked herself to the hospital. She said she found me in a basket.

I was born on October 2, 1990, in Nanjing, China. My father was not there for my birth. My father waited for me to be born but left when I didn't come out. My mother has a long scar from where I, or they, cut her.

I was born a girl and I was born a boy.

I was born on October 3, in the seventies, in the fourth-largest city of my parents' province. My father stayed for my birth but I didn't show up. When I did—my mother still has a scar. I left on a plane when I was four and a half. Saw my father for the first time when we landed. When I grew up, I forgot his birthday, he told me he made up the date of his birthday, so I don't know whether I forgot the lie or the real thing.

I was born as my father, who died in the womb.

I was born on October 4, 1990, in Shanghai, China, the only child of my parents. My parents met in silence, I imagine them laughing, rarely did they laugh together in memory but this doesn't mean it didn't happen.

I was born on October 5, in the eighties, in the second-largest city of my parents' province. My mother was twenty-seven, only a month apart from my father. Later, we moved to Canada. My mother worked in the back of a Chili's to learn English. My father learned English by eating the nightly mozzarella sticks. We cooked cats with neighbors and friends. I kept jars and jars of grasshoppers. My parents grew more than a month apart. My father named me for a bird, then disappeared into migration.

Listening to Teresa Teng

in a poem that is not yet good.
I am not yet good

in the home my parents made
to survive a little more familiarly.

My parents don't know what they want.
I know what they want and I know

I won't give it to them. Inheritance,
or what to do with knowledge.

It calls me. I have to sing it out.

Tenants

My mother wants me to know that she drank a bottle of water in the hotel room and that I might be charged for it. Drinking a bottle of water in a hotel room. A hotel being where we buy the right to stay still when no place will stay for us. On my way to the airport to pick up my mother, I carry a meal that may be light enough for after a flight. When the body is put into motion, it is not still. My mother's body has been in motion for fourteen hours and what can we eat after that. My mother's body never stops. My mother's body doesn't own anything, not even the motion it is put into.

Flight

Once, you dove
through ice
to prove
what you'd do
for your family.

What would I do
for my family?

What I ask from disappearance
is that I don't have to do it again.

Blackout

Wake in the middle
of the night to turn
off the lights
that have turned
back on. Then
in pitch dark
witness the riffing
cicadas with the finger
of my brow. Roving
through the wind
beating against rock
and brush. I could
die here. Gone
as lucent rush,
star of cold
dominoing
land I love.

III

Antiaubade

I love waking up at 6am.
   I love the early birds.
   I love the long dark of the winter day,
      the never-ending plumpness of summer.
Severe and quiet, loving and ministered
           by light.
   Both beautiful.

I have not written in months and months.
What will I do about it but slowly
   go further back into where I left off?

                I cannot fear
my own face, knowing its alterations.

Reconstruction

Do not grow flowers
in the valley of my breasts.

Slip the muck until it
learns to lick and multiply.

Chew each root to the
last sinew still mangled
and attached to me.

In a spew of yellow pus,
I am crowned with my wound.

No, I am not so generous.
What I've tried to touch,
I had no capacity.

All my life, I believed I was the cruel one.
I couldn't say what I believed. I lived it.

Catullus 85

And I can make it more complicated.
I can make it more about how I loved
you, you hated that I loved you, I loved
you so I hated that I loved
you with you, I never hated
that you hated that I loved
you, but I hated that I loved
you because you hated

it, until I hated
it, until I hated
how I made it—that I loved
you with what you hated,
until I hated why I loved
it, not you, but all of it.

The Friend

A public road.

A man at a tea shop that doesn't exist saw a woman and an other woman. He heard everything the woman said to the other woman: this woman was saying *Fuck you* and *How dare you* louder and louder, and then later on the street. The man at the tea shop wasn't there when the woman screamed at the other woman on the street. The man at the tea shop wasn't there when the woman said to the other woman that the tea shop wasn't there.

A *friend*.

With a handful of raspberries
in my hand, a voice is asking me,

in my head, why I don't include
the bad things.

I say it's because I don't want violence to be beautiful.
That I am responsible to what I make beautiful.

But does beauty have anything to do
with violence and what's made of it?

A friend.

I don't remember which episode
of the R. Kelly documentary
I am watching with my sister.
Andrea Kelly, his now-ex wife, tells
a story of how she was told to stay
in her room while he watched
a basketball game with guests.
She is getting hungry but
doesn't have permission to leave
the room. Sparkle hears a strange
knocking over the basketball
and wonders what it is,

but Robert doesn't notice.
Sparkle notices. Andrea
trying to get permission.
The door opens—

Oh, that's right. Andrea Kelly doesn't tell this story. It's Sparkle
    who tells this story.
When Andrea Kelly tells a story, she will start to cry—

the dark place stays where
the dark still plays in her mind.

The friend.

It is spring and all the buds
have bloomed.

I enter the kitchen and there is silence
except for you talking to your friend
who is also my friend. Silence means

I am now unseen.
We are getting groceries. I follow you
to your car, into the backseat
where your dogs are kept. You keep

talking to your friend
who is also my friend.
He talks back to you.
I lean forward. My voice lingers

but it leaves the car.

o

When I walk behind you two
to the grocery store, I still don't know
what I have done. There
the produce glistens louder
than I am to the universe.

o

To your friend
who is also my friend,
you aren't silent

when you talk to him.
                        I am.
If I'm heard, it is only
                        the car.
If I'm seen, it is only
                        the produce moving.

                o

In the kitchen, we are making
dinner, your friend who is also
my friend tells us both to
stop fighting, but I am not
fighting. I am noticing

where I don't exist.
I should leave. But

when we move,
it's to the den to watch a show.
I try but can't stomach the episode.

                o

What is it that happens
when you whisper across
the den, striking
match after match,
a fire now swelling
on the tongue?

Somehow it goes from what I did
to you breaking me down like a stick
for the flame.

What I did to you always deserved this.
What you did to me was this.

o

What I did: I brought you raspberries.

o

I'll go to sleep. Before night seethes
past your darkening corridor.

o

We get to the room and I'm dared
to agree: you're the monster.
I neither lie nor tell the truth
for both of us. And very precisely
you tell me there's a bus that runs
early in the morning
if I don't want you

to drive me. Very precisely
I think about this bus in the dream
I don't leave.

o

Somehow it goes from you asking me
again what it is I want from you
and me not remembering if I said

nothing: only the feeling of my throat
swollen and my head beating in
silence I can't talk myself out of.

What did I want from you
but not this? Then you daring me
to call you a monster and me saying no,

that's not it. I don't ask for it,
but you circle facts about the morning
bus that doesn't require you to drive me,

then reenter the dark. And your friend
who's my friend is in the den
still enjoying the show.

o

I can't stomach the episode. I'll go to sleep.
So you lead me through the dark corridor.

Unprompted: *You thought you would sleep
in my room?*

The point is not the question:
it is the silent answer *(How dare you)*.

You leave me in this other room
at 11pm. It is your house. I doze

beneath the covers, teeth chattering
until I try to stop listening. Above,

the sound of the show which is loud
enough for you and your friend

who is also my friend.
You are my friend. And I hate

how I can't sleep in the cold.
And I hate having to emerge

from the corridor
just to ask for something warm.

o

But no one who loves me hears
exactly what you're saying to me.
No one who loves me is here
to hear what I say back,
and even I've forgotten myself

speaking. Would they cover their ears,
ashamed of how *I* am comforting *you*?
Or would they help me move?

o

You lead me back through the door.
You hand me a sweatshirt that is yours
and you want nothing to do with it.

It is not even dark in the night
until you switch off the light
to emerge in the light.

o

Within the year
     (you scream at me over text,
     then in whispers, then on the phone,
     then on the street—with stories,
     with politics, with love, with anger,

with tears—then finally
cruelly, then not remembering)

I disappeared.

o

It is spring. The buds must have bloomed
in the cold.

It is a year before we separated.
You were my friend.

The Cliff

The dream is long and I have already forgotten.
We look to sit near the water but the water rushes over the seats.
Dream you sneers at me, saying
why would anyone want to be with someone
who couldn't say enough of the right things.
Of course, there is no such thing as enough. Of course,
there is no water. There are words that,
if I say them in the right tones and sounds,
will be sufficient for this to quiet down.
Dream me trying to pull together

the perfect words.
Waking me says this too:
I miss you, I love you more than anything.

And I have to live with my love.
It is almost more painful than the pain itself.

Eurydice at the Mouth

This is how I led myself out of a place so dark
that when I looked back, I could not see it,
or refused to see it.

These words came as water, my body writ
in water, turning through memory in search
of the lapidary inscription—the answer
and what binds me to my death.
If I will find it; if I will let it drown;

if I will use it to write this instead.
What would it be to match the depths of hell
with my own light, made and mangled as
a beast that bites both what is good and evil?

Fingers groping for a face through the black
and invisible. Wet feet clawing
on the maw of the underworld.

I was a woman, I suffered, I was there.
It is late where you are and where I come from.

Aubade (Two of Cups)

Waking up together, gray and annulated in not-yet-dawn.
Moving and closed in grooves of lap and arm-stretch.
Tell me what you've come to dream, your first breaths
since water, Lethe, your strokes with the dead.
Who you visited, I'll hear about. Pull you back to bed.

Home for the Holidays

It is possible that the implement meant to create ease is actually one that promotes discomfort. Case in point: my laptop resting on the tray in front of me forces me to raise my arms uncomfortably in order for me to write and think and search for whatever it is I am doing on the laptop. The laptop, now comfortably on my lap, wishes me well, moves slightly over my legs in bed, the bed I've been in since approximately this morning eight days ago.

This morning, I watched my body being undressed as if for the first time. In a way, it was the first time. Two tubes hung listlessly from my side, clipping, finally, to two suctioning bulbs on my pants. Which were, at various points this week, filled with blood and pus. The tubes on my side are next to two yellow foam bolsters sewn into my chest, above what I would today begin calling my nipples.

For over a week, I had been gingerly moving around these bolsters, the incisions on my chest like two shut eyes never to waken again, deep black lines made of other black lines. My chest sewn into my chest, every minute or so feeling like a cactus growing out of itself, invisible, thin-headed needles pricking out of my skin. Or so is the rush of skin connecting again with skin.

My body below all these bandages, glue, tape. Blood where the drains went into my body caked and even grafted to my skin: splinters that had sunk so far I could see only the shadow of them. Susan exclaimed, this afternoon, about the miracle of the body feeling an enormous amount from glass in one's foot.

Skin again, attached to nothing, can reattach. The body is greedy with itself. These two sides of skin began to confuse each other. One became the other, and vice versa.

Skin again, reattached, below my bolsters, the sponged keepers of what I would soon begin to call my nipples, revealing two wet patches like the spread of a baby's forehead when first revealed from the womb. The body reinventing itself became again its own mystic. That's a medical term, my doctor said, the term being something I don't remember as she picked away from my nipple, pink-gray and still internal, emerging from viscous. I looked on with revulsion and shock and barely breathed, which is how, I suppose, people pass out while looking at their own new bodies.

My doctor did many things and said much, picking out the stitches from my body, the rest to be dissolved, and me, *à bout de souffle* above; bacitracin, dabbing, drains, holes, blood, counting to three and coughing and the cogent rumble of left chest letting out some warm froth and tubing.

Of the time we're awake, we remember the heat, and to me it was to be touched but from the inside, my own muscle being rubbed from behind, the inevitable mess of what followed it on the patient robe below me. The tube now resting behind me, we did the other side. I had to take a breath for what felt like an eternity. Again: breathing; rumble; tubes; wanting to be free of them but also to never be moved again.

In the midst of all that, I felt myself pouring out merely, probably, a dribble, quite unlike what I have heard it is like to bring forth a living human into the world. My body, which delivered itself, the medicant and medicated. What low rushing would I be able to see, my pale nipples, the closed eyes of my chest, two sets of eyes now, four eyes, my scars enabling me to be doubly alive.

In one week, I will feel the phantom pang of my previous nipples, eyes opened to the air they are. I dress.

Detail

I'm wiping the glue off an old book,
a fact so small who knows if I would have
told it to you. Afterward, there continue
these accumulations. We woke at this time
and spoke first to each other each day
for three years,
and now what?

I was in love and once illuminated.
Now I am alone. Peddling in plain morning
like a god who walks toward a street of only
birds. Only in their singing do they fly apart
and grow their understanding.

Spring of Cups

The people we love disappear before our eyes.
We can't follow or know where they go.
They lose the names we have known them by

slowly and slowly, the dance which turns
until their names are gone
and the people we love have disappeared.

Will they choose new names before they go
into the arms of other lovers or other homes
we can't know or follow? Wherever they go

there are flowers standing in their hair
or ripples coined around their stares,
and the people we love will disappear.

We do the dance before we find
the other gone.
We lose the places we have known them by.

The person I love disappears before my eyes.
How long have I taken to know you?
            How far will you take your name?
I can't follow or know. You go away.

Perennation

It is loudly, as if the mind wakes.
The lily swelling suddenly in the dark.
From its center stands a rustic tongue
dashed with moonwater. Pungent
on its axle, steady in its pooling, where
I lay toward its opening. All around
the violets undisturbing any scent
of stamen in my mouth, fully curling.

IV

Affirmation

A quiet night home.
But am I lonely?
Next to me, a   new set of green and red candles
glowing.

Keeping everything together,   disposing of what I don't
need.
I sense and hear the change.

                                                                    Yet
          I still want some kind of contact. Yet
I am the one who can't let go
                    —into complete silence,
          which seems so unthinkable. What keeps me?
          Is it devotion or addiction? Is it the need for
          intimacy, or the proof that I can survive
          some kind of violence?

          All kinds.
          The candles light the ground, are red and green.
          Christmas colors, my favorite season, a
          joyful time of year.

          Together, inside.   I turn away

to what is impossible to ask for—easy love.

Balenciaga

Beyond the sanctuary sprang the train,
ruin in white.
The train's lank hood.
I thought I saw you in the hood
that pushed out the light.
It was us I saw

in the sanctuary. There
the lonely fall away
through the middle of the aisle.
No bells, no singing,
for as long as waiting
adamants.

It is not like betrotheds hiding
on the night before, but
that we truly don't know each other.

Faith

There is no majestic horn that sounds
the end of battle. There is no majesty
in battle. Only knowing, abruptly, as if
a curtain's been drawn, the actors
are not coming back to life. Knuckles
swollen and out of proportion. Giving in
to how it must go on — our arms shuffling
out the bodies, the tightness of our hips
and knees carrying the blood away from
the ground so useless to the vessels now.
I remember sitting by the window of my last
place, trying to understand. Not believing
it was over. Hating always being told
about who I was and being hated
for being the one told. As usual I was
the last to know not because I was stupid,
but because of what I wanted to exist.

Paradise, Lost

                  Standing where the village just awakened,
                  just the shops and couples taking pictures
                  in the most beautiful place

on earth,
the bougainvillea
flaring deeply.

                  Not yet, still darker, all very sudden
                  wanting to speak

again.
Wet air
cleft by
heat and cold
collected bare

                  on liters of water. Then waiting
                  for the bus to Akrotiri, but following
                  a woman calling

Monolithos.
Monolithos,
for black sand
and charred fish

                  with a thirst of no brilliance.

Monolithos,
the sound
of her voice —

                  I want to be beautiful
                  and a part of this earth.

Migrants

To drift is not surrender.
The backwards call of a bird
is the sound of another bird.

Things We Didn't Know

The moon's white tusk
behind the trees is a *lune*.
Its effect is the French
of its English.

The trees are standing
though they must lie down,
and in my body I know
the sea is bobbing.

I am watching news in
every block's receding rooms.
The streetlights slink like the fox
who sleuthed before the cross

in the garden.
And in my body I know
as though my legs are planted
firmly in the sound

the fog is breathing on the waves.
The trees are standing
though they must lie down.
I will never be the same.

Home for the Holidays

Now somewhere else, I have become more greedy. I no longer want to live another life but to inhabit at least two lives in one. One in which I was myself before these two years and another in which I am only the self I have been since those years have passed. It does not allow for, for example, the facts of my existence, my comforts, the responses of my body, the sense that my body holds for me more than I know how to remember. I dream (primarily in the day) about how I'll awake with my body in the moment I was on the operating table, completely outside the room. I gave its pulse to other people and I must always ask: was it worth this life to trade it for another life? What continuity is there between a body that is less and less recognizable in one life and then another? Is this truly the same body, or have I even exceeded the body I thought I would reach?

Ting was with me today. My two good memories of Ting are one night more recently of them breezing in on a Citi Bike, for dinner, and another, in which they had different hair, dancing to Willow, their body ecstatic under the lights. One wonders how we have and allow others to have memories of our selves passed: may I have both portraits of Ting, who is still wholly the same person and yet completely different, wondering, groping somewhere past the places that we societally may see or agree as radical?

While somewhere else, my mother doesn't recognize my new voice on the phone. She panics and tries to call me again. I say I am sick. Which is not the first time. The first time, I was also sick. I am getting further and further from this imprint of myself, an image I never believed in, an imprint I pushed myself into so someone else could have room. In one life I have become sick and in this one I am becoming better and better. I need to be sick to be well. My two sets of eyes beginning to make sense of their sights. My two eyes double-exposing on each other, the dream on the reality, the ordinary aspect leaning over a puddle of its own confounding.

Making Double

In Zen Buddhism, every ritual is a form. If the form is successful, it becomes a mirror. In the mirror, I see who I am, my thoughts and hopes, my desires and unremarkable pleasures. I was a mirror and unremarkable, too, to those I loved. On the one hand, the fear that I wasn't acceptable enough to keep around; the need to hide behind the thoughts and wishes of another person. On the other hand, the gift of revealing someone to themself. I have been resented and loved for all the same things: listening, waiting, the ability to hear, sometimes too well. Today, on my way to the train, I hear this again: if the form is successful, it becomes a mirror. And the mirror, this self, is valuable and perfected over lifetimes longer and more various than, and including, my own.

V

Ambulance! Ambulance!

When Love flung round the corner
all the fruits on the corner flung
their colors at his feet, the rebel windows
spread their arms and rejoiced in daylight
and I stood with my heart on a platter
of asphalt and its near white lines. O Love
left me stuck between the teeth of the neon
traffic porter commanding me to
STOP—then I pirouetted against the line
in my trench coat which is more romantic

than jaywalking alone in tennis shoes.
Love caught me alive and I caught him too
and smacked his bright cheeks
when he asked for it (saying *thank you,
Daddy*) and tied the knots, moaning something
awful while the neighbor couples kept going
on with their business not knowing who
we were. Love with his shoulder
bag of prairie shoots as light as a pack of
darts in a basement bar—red and dim

as the tips, those nights, Love in the
bathroom not watching couples kiss
for the first time in a lesbian bar always
the last of its kind. And we'd stop at
the pier after staring in Chelsea at the
new art we hoped would understand
us. Then a long walk from the subway
to my house with Swiss chard I've wrapped

from the farmers market and always baby's
breath or yellow sunflowers which I can't get

enough of—Love, how do we grow tall
like them? Or like me, small at the Met,
staring at the fountain in the Japanese
Gallery drawing the waves and waiting
for Love to tap and feed me marble grapes.
I've never made it to Fire Island but I hope
to be as warm one day as sand untouched
by human ass. People walk on this beach
exchanging looks perfectly timed in search
of Love, while sun will fill with even more

of who is capable of missing us. Like Love,
I was young when I died to my family.
I forget from the beginning and remember
the end, then the days after where the future
is buzzing with half-shaved heads,
mine and Love's alone, Love who walked
and held my hand in a field of strobe lights,
uncertain mauve shuffling in The Year of Our
Love, the orange poppies announcing it was
The Year of Our Love, their eyes as juiced

as the mandarins questing for their origins
if they could remember past their trundling
pasts, too. And when Love came calling there
were strawberries in the rose bouquet. I hid
behind a tree standing straight as possible
and stared at its back prancing on the crosswalk.

I wanted to be worth Love's time but I was not
ready. There I was before Love gluing shards
of broken windows into a chandelier; before
Love smoothing a branch with the bright

edge of a stone; before Love baking box cakes,
labeling entire libraries just my name while
listening to music as though my silent head
could make the honey that would bring
Love over. I prayed and I summered
before Love stayed and Love went. Remember
when I'd give up Love to be held on another
continent? Remember my bells from the Orient,
my almond lips synced to Robyn on the Amtrak?
Missing, perhaps, *je ne sais quoi?* Was that Love?

Love watched me watch my mother eating
nonchalantly when we ordered too much,
the old memories of someone stern softening
as the rice in good congee (and yes, we had it),
wondering when it would get the same dignity
as a thousand-year egg or its immortality.
A thousand years is still a death anyway.
My grandpa's smoking on the balcony
for the next thousand years, the same cigarette
because he thinks if he slows it'll last. I went out

to his funeral finally, last, because I was not
always ready, and the processional began
inside me on this day with very bold tears.
I last saw Love marching out with the same

slouch and cigarette he'd never light as a way
to start quitting, how he'd quote Rimbaud
or nutritional boasts on cereal boxes, and then
on the day he died: stabbed in broad daylight
trying to cross the street by you,
my love, who didn't give a damn.

四川话

Winter mornings
I'd wake to my parents
murmuring downstairs:
their voices not gentle,
but following the natural
glides of their own deer.
Waking knowing no one
would come up, but some
days I would be called from
the bottom of the stairs.
Just my name in a dialect
that looked like us.
That it was time for school.
That they were leaving,
but that they'd wait for me.
How embarrassed I was
for them to sound
of a country that only
we knew. Years later,
I sat on a bus with a girl
who was born here. We'd
known each other a year.
But only alone could we
have asked ourselves
where we were *really* from.
Then struck, lightning
through our fawnish
mouths, having reached
the same province we both
weren't willing to seek

or reveal. Grateful, for those
mornings in bed, hearing
my mother at the foot
of the stairs, even though
I couldn't reach her.

Lengthening, Rites

There is nothing quite as lovely as after the winter solstice, the days getting longer, and the sun of spring wrapping a glove over the room. The room which is sometimes a kitchen, a classroom, a place to sleep. I can't stop singing praises of this daily peace, this wash of visibility. As the details of the room make way for leafless branches wafting away, then back. Adrienne Rich in my lap. The clock striking each second above a large copy of "Toward the Solstice." From the blushed velvet to the woven fabric across the glass coffee table, my eyes lay there. Even sleep could not catch me here.

What were those days? Gilded and bare, laughing on a street corner with Anthony. With Kate at tea; with Kate and her poem about lemons, about breath and shucked skin. Those days when I stank of sun and lilacs. Those days of candlelit reading, drinking too much, thinking in my stupor I could write. In the mornings, rather, the poems were there. They didn't need to be written.

Dream of the Divided Field

The relation between what we see and what we know is never settled.
—John Berger, *Ways of Seeing*

Grief paralyzes. Motion continues; time departs.
Something's left with no means to retrieve it.
A candle out in the down-clap of darkness. Then to wade
      and wade —

In grief: I, detached from place and time.

o

You appear in candlelight across the table.
The oysters gleam in butter. I ask for your hand.
Our fingers hold together for the first time.

o

*If we accept that we can see that hill over there, we propose that
from that hill we can be seen.*

o

In a voicemail, you're walking downhill
to your house, a detail I now know about.

Static crinkles out your breath
to see if I want to talk.

o

I worry that your dream was right.
That I was the abuser, not you. How do I know?

o

We only see what we look at. To look is an act of choice.

o

There's a way, in your dream,
that you're able to love me.

The you I love inside the dream
who asks how we can remember.

I want your dream to be right.

o

Now somewhere else, when I read your words,
I get back into the habit of undoing my own.

o

I said yes to your dream so many times
I saw myself as you dreamed me.

o

*If we can see the present clearly enough, we shall ask the right
questions of the past.*

o

How do I know?
I don't.

o

Once you leave someone, the dream becomes divided.
Your sense of reality. Their sense of reality.

o

*Images were first made to conjure up the appearances of
something that was absent.*

o

The divided field is a field that cannot be seen
through the eyes of one person. That is,
a field with space for your absence.

o

In my dreams, you remain as vivid as ever,
but you no longer have control over me.

o

A dream is in and out of focus; it is both to aspire
and to touch in spirit—reverie. It is the act of giving
away control of consciousness, to see and be seen
but out of focus. A dream is, in both cases, a vision.

The dream reminds me: what I see and what I know
are never settled. The dream is, also, neither the future
nor the past but a perception of the world through me,
both voluntary and not.

It was voluntary: I followed the feeling.
But *to hear correctly is my concern. I have no other.*
So what is written follows, gets lost, finds the path
again—and what is seen there: that is all included.

The End of Another Year

Simply, a little after 5pm. Thinking
about island time: time which is not quite time.
I am on an island. Waking this morning
to the east of me — clouds are still moving
even though they do so covering the sky.
Whether or not I could see beyond them
was not the point. Time was just
an assurance that it was passing: life,
these increments, scuttling continuously
in a line. My heavy curtain, burgundy red, left
folded to the wayside, and a window naked.
Streetlights no longer bother me,
or the sound. I haven't been woken
in ages. In one dream I could live a hundred lives
and, no matter, that has already passed,
when I blinked each dream already
receding, though as I closed my eyes
there was still the logic of their absences,
the roads on which they'd go. And I, too,
could go on. Should I choose to sleep.
My eyes closed. Again, the batting mist,
gliding water passing by the rotating travelers.
Like machines, it was what we would call them,
not what they did. I gave away my eyelids.
I peeled away the absinthe of the dreams
where I lived not for one night
but for my life. I dreamed, then island time.
As if forgetting, not wanting, to go or be
anywhere. That nothing mattered
but the rhythm of should I sleep or should I wake.
Nobody to be with. Nowhere to go.

Instead, that vast stillness, where air becomes
heavy as hands pressing upon my swollen chest
breaking out of itself. It did not matter what time.
I could come and go as I pleased between this life
and the other. Later, taking in tea, I would also
enter another. Later, at my desk, on my futon,
the fabric and the platform, that my body
could be lifted through sheer fact of resistance.
It happens all the time. I am a beast of two worlds.
A swollen chest infinitely smaller
than another one, this etched chest whose face
I still don't know the heat of.
Where I wept, there was transformation.
And I did both before and after
I flew through the other worlds. In the apse
where I slept, nobody came, and I caved,
my two eyes blind, now covered, now obsolete.
Where I went, the world was full of more
order, new homes, new glass. On the island
where nothing mattered, I stepped closer
to the crystal of my wanting,
that dissipate mist, that grandiose clap.
I dreamt and woke up. I passed
my life into my life, and gave
one clock for another.
It was as if I had no memories
but a clanging recognizance: on my own,
at sea, the port getting faded where I stared—
where I was out of breath and in of air.

Deconstruction

If it was you I loved,
then I merely imagined

a dream with no borders.
I imagined the black-

birds, sleek and heavy
in the rain. The train

in the distance, orange
and smoking, disguised

the ricketing horizon.
I imagined the day.

I imagined the night, too,
white ships passing

for delivery trucks
breathing heavy in

the peat. Of our stillness,
I imagined our dreaming,

then waking in the middle
of the night, you whispering

your dream of a man
laughing and men

laughing on the sidewalk
outside. When I touched

your face, it was a shadow,
for I even imagined

the darkness we received
at night, your nightly fear

of disappearing a shadow's
fear of disappearing, too,

and I assured you, we were not,
for I imagined both, the fear

and the disappearance,
warm light in the kitchen

not a coat hook, not shoes,
not keys,

not wanting to leave.
And where you have gone,

are there hours
where I disappeared, too?

Yes, I imagined us
laughing. I was not a man,

but a blackbird cawing
before departure,

the train getting darker,
an antic twilight going farther

than the dark-imagined sky
imagining heat, imagining ardor,

imagining so much wanting
to be moved by love.

I Had a Vision of a Hill

and a love with red and brown
hair. The hair being part of mine or
theirs. The hill being no one's.

Marriage is not knowing who
will own the land, or ever.
I had a vision of a hill.

Garden Sketch

On the left hand corner is
the bottom mound, surrounded
by dense shrubbery. Over the mound
to the right is the beginning
of the land, which stretches
further than itself in an ecstatic
flailing. The land is cornered
by only what is necessary,
its bare back. It goes on and on
to the middle, which: only what
we have been able to re-create
here in this space. Peel the corners;
there is laughing. But no people.
The sun appears in the lower right
corner while its gaze goes on dotting
to the moon surely rising (top right).
In the middle of the land is a lake.
And then in its middle a man.
That is me. I look back at you.

Aubade

    I woke up with so much love for you
It doesn't matter where I am

I am making eggs

    The sun is warming my just-shaved head
like your hand when sometimes
                    it rests there

Translation

In the Roman room, the columns
were bright in their patience.
I warmed my pate on the marble wall.
My mind returned to me.
For years the coolness softened
what was known as my interior.
I was fortunate in that way.
Still able to love soon after
I gave myself away.
Something held up
inside, ungraceful or even
formal. Not forceful. Not I.
There was one among
the rooms remaining,
recognizing me. Wanting
me to stay. And to admit
I was the original.

Once

I admit it.
That we were alive
at once
the same time.

That we were connected
to each other.
And two minds

move me
as this life
becomes a story.

We were alive,
we were free,

choosing the hour
within a moment's

bright precision.
There is still that hour

without a future or a face.
I am the hour. I am the place.

Notes

"Family Tree" is after Luc Sante's "Résumé." Thank you to Wo Chan for introducing me to this piece.

"Listening to Teresa Teng" uses the common English name for the Taiwanese singer 邓丽君 as it appears on Spotify.

"Catullus 85" is a slant translation of the titular poem.

"The Friend": "A public road" is the setting of Act 4, Scene 5, of *The Taming of the Shrew*; "A friend" (second section) refers to episode 2 of the docuseries *Surviving R. Kelly*.

"Eurydice at the Mouth" modifies a line from Whitman: "I am the man, I suffered, I was there."

Both "Aubade (Two of Cups)" and "Spring of Cups" refer to the tarot suit of cups.

"Balenciaga" is after the 1967 wedding dress by House of Balenciaga, on view at the Metropolitan Museum of Art Cloisters during the spring 2018 "Heavenly Bodies" exhibition.

"Paradise, Lost": Monolithos is the village in Santorini where poets Linda Gregg and Jack Gilbert lived together for some time.

"四川话" is after Robert Hayden's "Those Winter Sundays."

"Dream of the Divided Field": Italicized quotes are from *Ways of Seeing* by John Berger. The quote in the last section is from an essay by Marina Tsvetaeva, translated by Angela Livingstone.

"Once" is after Sappho 51.

Acknowledgments

The poems in this collection have appeared previously, in various forms, in the following journals and anthologies:

Academy of American Poets' *Poem-a-Day*: "Landscape with a
    Hundred Turns"
Already Felt: Poems in Revolt & Bounty: "Aubade (Two of Cups)"
Bellevue Literary Review: "Taking Care"
Cellpoems: "Migrants"
Memorious: "Eurydice at the Mouth"
New England Review: "Catullus 85," "Detail," "Dream of the
    Divided Field"
Queenzenglish.mp3: "Family Tree"
Reservoir: "Aubade," "Listening to Teresa Teng"
The Shade Journal: "Flight"
West Branch: "Home for the Holidays"

Thank you to James Merrill House, Asian American Writers' Workshop, and Millay Colony for the Arts for the time and space some of these poems occupy.

Thank you to my agent, Rebecca Nagel, for your tireless support and advocacy throughout this book's journey.

Thank you to Nicole Counts, for your belief and time in talking out and working on the shape and message of its final form. Thank you to the whole team at One World, who moved this book into physical, public existence.

Thank you to Elizabeth Onusko, Michelle Meier, Rebecca Ariel Porte, and Emma Healey for your detailed feedback, friendship, and encouragement during various stages of this book.

Thank you to HK for your steadfast love and care.

As I think about those for whom I felt so much gratitude while writing this book, I wonder if there is a difference between those who gave me guidance on where to go with my art and on where to go with my survival.

Thank you.

About the Author

YANYI is a writer and critic. He is the author of *The Year of Blue Water*, winner of the 2018 Yale Series of Younger Poets Prize. His work has been featured on NPR's *All Things Considered*, in *Tin House, Granta, A Public Space*, and at the New York Public Library, and he has received fellowships from Asian American Writers' Workshop and Poets House. Currently, he is poetry editor at *Foundry* and giving creative advice at *The Reading*.

YANYIII.COM

TWITTER: @YANYI___

INSTAGRAM: @YANYI.DOCX